HIGH INCOME SKILLS SECRET

Discover The Four Little-Known High Income Skills That's Turning Yearly Income Into Monthly Income For Ordinary persons In This Digital Economy

Copyright © 2017 Grand write

All rights reserved. No part of this publication may be reproduced, distributed, or transmitted in any form or by any means, including photocopying, recording, or other electronic or mechanical methods, without the prior written permission of the publisher, except in the case of brief quotations embodied in critical reviews and certain other noncommercial uses permitted by copyright law. For permission requests, write to the publisher.

Table of Contents

HIGH INCOME SKILLS SECRET............................1

SKILLS TO DEPLOY......9

  People's Problem Mining Skill:................................9

  Solution Discovery Skill: 12

  Sellduction Skill:............17

  Traffic generation skill:. 19

Hello

Congratulations for getting this ebook,

In this very book, am gonna be revealing to you 4 little-known high income skills that ordinary persons are using today to turning their once yearly income to now monthly income.

Am gonna be making this book very short but at the same time I will be revealing secret information that will completely transform your finances should you run with them, What am about revealing to you is what took me from earning #42,000 per month, and #500,000 per year to now making #500,000 per month, and some months more than that, yeah.

So read this ebook till the end. Some few years ago, while I was reading one book like that which one of my mentors gave me, I came across one statement that completely changed my life forever, In that book, I read something that says - "Your income will hardly rise above you skill level or your personal development".

Now pause and reread that last paragraph again, this time read it slowly and allow it to sink in.

Have you done that?

Good Now let me explain, Now as you reading this ebook right now, I don't know how much you making per year right now, But let's assume it's #1,200,000, that's #100,000 monthly, Hear this, You are able to generate that amount because of the problems you are solving that's getting people give you their money, And you are able to solve those problems because of the skills and resources that you possess, So for you to transform from making that your 1.2 million yearly income into your monthly income, All you have to do is simply get high income skills that generates like 1.2 million per month and not per year, Bu I want to ask you, do you believe that there are skills like that, I mean do you believe that there are high income skills that can generate like 1.2 million in a month? Well if you don't believe that, I would advise you to look around you and see that people are making such amount in a day, not

even month, But if you look around you and you didn't see such kind of persons, then you are in the wrong environment, take a leave, you are not tree, you are not planted there, Know why am telling you to change environment? Because this money making thing, from my own experience is 95% mindset and 5% what you do, Now if I guessed correctly, you are now asking, what are examples of this 1.2million/per month high income skills and how do I possess it? Stay with me here, I will tell you, But before I do that, Ever since I read about that statement which is that your income will hardly rise above your skills level, I took skill acquisition, I mean personal development very seriously, When I say skills, I don't mean anyhow skills though, rather am talking about High Income Skills, And one of the things I will continue doing till the day I die is investing in my personal development, Now hear this, Investing in your personal development Is the best form of investment because it pays very high return on investment, Now talking about investing in personal development, I am suppose to charge you for the information am about revealing to you right now, But please, don't allow the fact that you got this ebook for free make you not to value it, please resist that temptation, Having said that, Let's get right into it, The first skill is.....

SKILLS TO DEPLOY

People's Problem Mining Skill:

For you to make a whole lot of money, you must start with this skill, You want to master how to mine for people's problem like they mine for gold, Yes, people's pressing problems can become a goldmine for you to make money, This is so because, when you really take a cursory look at it, the money you looking for right now is in other people's pocket and bank accounts, And the only thing that will make them bringing it out to give you is if you are gonna help them solve that their pressing problem. There is no other way to make money aside uncovering people's problems, in otherwords their wants and needs and helping them satisfy it. The money you are looking for right now is in other peoples bank accounts, wallets and pockets, isn't it? And now if you don't want to carry gun,

which I wouldn't advise you to do, The other way you can use to getting them give you that their money aside from pointing gun at them is to find one pressing problem that they are going through, Let me give you an example, Imagine a woman who is struggling to get the fruit of the womb, she hasn't given one child for her husband, and the mother in-law is on her neck pressuring her to prove that she truly has a womb, pressuring her to give her a child, You will agree with me that such a woman wouldn't be sleeping at night with her two eyes closed, will she? That's a pressing problem, What about a man who is not satisfying her woman in bed and he is gradually losing her respect, she is even threatening to go outside, how do you think the man will be feeling? He will be feeling bad, isn't it, Now what about a young man who is doing a 9-5 job, that they are paying him 45k per month, he wakes up by 4 am every morning so that he can beat the Lagos traffic to get to work early and he gets home by 10pm each day, His salary get spent even before he receives it, his aged parents are on his neck to send them some money for upkeep, How do you think that man would be fairing, Now those I listed up there are pressing problem, you need to get discovering this pressing problems as a skill. It will change your life as it did change mine. But when you uncover a pressing problem, do you know what you want to do with it? Come with me,

Solution Discovery Skill:

This is another skill that many don't know about that will make you a whole lot of money, remember the first skill I told you about is the problem mining skill, where I told you that you need to learn and master how to uncover peoples pressing problem, Uncovering peoples problem is one thing, people are not gonna hand you over their money just because you know their problem, no my dear, They will happily hand you their money when you have the solution to that their pressing problem, money is only a medium of exchange, do not forget, What is the real value is the product or services that changes hands, people will always give you money when you have solution to their problem, Now question is how do you get this solution that you can offer this people suffering from one problem or the other so they can hand you that their money, There are many ways to do that, One is you can create the product yourself , it can be a physical product or digital product, When I talk about physical product, am talking about products like supplements, wristwatches, bags etc, But digital products are ones that are in digital format like ebooks, softwares, video courses, etc. Got it? The other way to get solution for people is to import already made products created by other persons and simply offer it to this persons suffering from the problem and collect their money legitimately with ease while they are smiling to you, Another way is to become an affiliate to another person's product, this simply involves you finding someone who has a product and you find those who needs it and you promote that product to them and when they buy the product using your unique affiliate link, you get paid handsome commissions, More on that later, I will be revealing to you how to start pocketing like 500k per month, doing this online business model called smart link sharing .

So uncovering peoples hot pressing problem will help you know what solution they are seeking for and you now mastering how to find a working product for them that will help them fix their problem is another skill many don't know about, And that skill will make you a whole lot of money, Let me give you an instance, let's say you uncovered a target audience for instance that are struggling with a particular problem, let's say it's the woman that is struggling to give birth, And you find a solution for them, maybe a working supplement from china, and you bring it down here and set up ads and target women who has that problem, Let's say you are buying that product for say #5000, you can sell it to them for #15000, when you minus the cost of product and cost of importing and running paid adverts to sell it, you will be left with say #8000 profit, If you sell 50 pieces of that particular product in a month, press your calculator and do the maths, Or let's say you selected the young guy who is struggling with a low paying job as your target audience, and you helped them find an affiliate product that teaches them how to start making say 500k per month on the internet without slaving for one greedy boss like that and without leaving their house, Let's say that affiliate product sells for say #20,000, and it pays affiliate agents 50%, 50% of 20000 is 10,000, isn't it? Now all you have to do to make 500k per month is to get like 50 persons buying that particular program and you will be smiling to the bank, Remember, finding this solution to a pressing problem that many people has, is a high income skill that no school will teach you, you can only learn it from me as you are learning right now in this ebook, That's the second skill that changed my life, Then the third skill you want to learn, which is the second to the last is......

Sellduction Skill:

You may be wondering which one is sellduction skill, I will answer, You are trying to get people hand you their money, do not forget that, Now at this point, you have uncovered a pressing problem for a particular audience, you have also discovered a product that solves that problem for them, One mistake I see many people making is they go telling people to buy the product they have for sale, don't do that, else you will struggle to make sales, Instead, what you want to do is master this next skill which I call sellduction skill, This skill will help you come up with something that will attract your target prospects, that is those who has the problem that you uncovered and that the solution you have picked helps solve, You want to master how to get this people coming to you not you chasing them, This is because when you go to people and tell them to buy, they will turn you down because humans are naturally selfish, they will think that you want to collect their money, But when you place a kind of bait that will attract them on their way just like where a fisherman places an earthworm attached to a hook to attract fishes while fishing, you can also find something that will serve like an earthworm to attract a particular target audience for whatever you want to sell, so that you will get this people coming to you and not you going or chasing them around, when they come to you, they give you the power to effortlessly sell to them, but when you chase them, you are giving them power to turn you down.

This is the skill of sellduction, when you master it, it will make you a lot of money because you will be selling effortlessly without being pushy like shitty sales people do, You will get people literally begging you to sell to them, If you would love mastering this sellduction high income skill, stay with me, am gonna be teaching you that, Then lastly, the other skill want to learn is the skill of…….

Traffic generation skill:

This one is the fourth skill that will help you earning big money when you learn it, But what is this traffic generation skill exactly? I will answer, But first, let me tell you what traffic is, traffic is simply a number of persons using the internet or visiting a particular web page or blog or youtube channel, That's what's called traffic, traffic = people. So you want to master how to drive a good number of persons to a product or services that you want sold, when you master that skill, it will get generating big money for you, even if you don't have your own product, you can drive traffic to other peoples product and get making commission maybe as an affiliate, Even if you don't have a capital to start up a business, if you master how to drive traffic, you will never be broke again in life, Here is how traffic generation skill will make you a lot of money, say you don't have a product of your own, You can simply find an affiliate product that solves a problem for a particular target audience, say underpaid employees, This affiliate product should be listed on an affiliate platform, Examples of affiliate platforms you can find affiliate products are: Lsearn.com,

Clickbank.com, Jvzoo.com, Digistore24.com Etc, When you go on those platform, simply get your unique link to that particular product and go find someone who needs that product and tell them something that will get them going to check out that product using your unique affiliate link, So when they checks it out and they buy, you will get paid commission, Say you selected a product that sells for #50,000 on an affiliate platform, and let's say that product pays 50% in commission, what that means is that should you get people checking that product, and they end up buying it, you will get paid 25k on each sales, And in a period of 30 days, if you get just 20 persons buying that product, you will be pocketing 500k, You see why traffic generation skill is such a high income skill you want to master, it changed my life, it is one of the skills that helped me turn my yearly income into my monthly income, it can do that for you too and it is doing for ordinary persons like us, So there you have it, That's the 4 little known high income skills that is helping ordinary people like me to become millionaires, turning our yearly income into our monthly income, If you would love to learn how to learn and master this skills, and turn your yearly income into your monthly income .

Hope you enjoyed reading this ebook as much as I enjoyed writing it for you, I didn't want it to be too long, I would have gone in detail to reveal some more stuffs to you about making a full time living online. All you have to do now is go watch that video and I will also keep in touch with you via messages and emails, so keep an eye on your email inbox.

My name is OGBE GIDEON You can reach me via this number should you need any help 08162513797.

See you at the ATM cash dispensing machines of this world. Congrats for reading

www.ingramcontent.com/pod-product-compliance
Lightning Source LLC
Chambersburg PA
CBHW070428240526
45472CB00020B/1711